'Remember him —
before the silver
cord is severed, or the
golden bowl is broken;
before the pitcher is
shattered at the spring,
or the wheel broken at
the well, and the dust
returns to the ground
it came from, and the
spirit returns to God
who gave it.

(Ecclesiastes 12:6-7)

In 2001 my mother visited us in Cambridge and, walking to church one Sunday, fell and broke her hip. From then on she died slowly and painfully over the next four and a half years. The pain was not physical so much as psychological, as she gradually lost all her freedom. As I watched her die, I prayed that I would not live into a similarly long and (through no fault of her own) increasingly incapacitated old-age, a burden to my wife and family, and an embarrassment to my friends, *'Sans teeth, sans eyes, sans taste, sans everything'*. I once said to the churchwardens at St Andrew the Great that I did not want to live to be a problem to those who cared for me: bad-tempered, irritable, snapping orders at my wife, Fiona, while she pushed me around in a wheelchair. One of the wardens replied that the only change would be the wheelchair!

Cancer

In the spring of 2007, while on sabbatical in New Zealand, I first had pains roughly in the area of the gallbladder, which led eventually to going into Addenbrooke's Hospital in December 2008 to have the gallbladder removed. But when he went in to do so, the surgeon found cancer which had invaded the liver, originating in the gallbladder.

The surgeon found cancer

It was past surgical solution and radiotherapy, and there was apparently no effective chemotherapy regime to cure gallbladder cancer. The oncologist estimated I might have six to nine months to live. My prayer when my

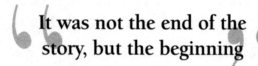

It was not the end of the story, but the beginning

mother died had been answered. I said to the surgeon when he broke the news, that what he had just told me was, for a Christian believer, not bad news but good; it was not the end of the story, but the beginning. (And I saw an imaginary speech bubble appear above his head, saying, "This man is in total denial!")

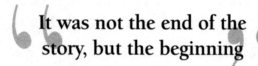

But I have lived 62 years of very happy life on the earth and, for over 40 of them, Jesus has been my Lord and my Saviour. So I can have no regrets. My main reaction was then, and remains now, one of gratitude. God *has* done all things well, and I believe he is doing this thing well too. He is taking me back to himself when I have all my faculties, when I am still active in ministry, when my family have reached independence with their own spouses and careers, and when my wife still has the energy and vitality to face a new life-stage.

Inevitable worries

There are inevitable worries. The financial provision for my wife as a clergy widow is bad (largely my own fault). Despite my huge inadequacies as a husband and a father, I fear my close family will miss me. But, taking all things into account, it is not a bad time to die.

And I have had warning. Once you have been told you are going to die, the months that follow are a very good time spiritually. The news is a spiritual tonic. *The long habit of living indisposeth us for dying*, wrote

Sir Thomas Browne; and for me as a
Christian that had certainly become

> **The months that follow are
> a very good time spiritually**

true. In many ways, I was more ready
to die on February 8th 1968 as a 20-
year old, the day after my conversion,
than I was in 2008 — 40 years later.

But the warning I have now received
has changed that. I can now see that
much of what I have strived for and
much of what I have allowed to fill my
life these 40 years has been of dubious
value. I am not now going to gain any
further reputation or achieve anything
more of significance, and I realise how
little that matters. As I start to clear

up my effects, I recognise how I have allowed them to clutter my life and how little I have actually needed them. While I would love to have provided better financially for my wife, I know that being 'comfortably provided for' will be of no spiritual help to her in the years ahead.

While physical things spoil and go dim, spiritual things grow brighter and clearer. I see my sin very clearly. I see how much it still controls my life. I think how little time I have got left to make further progress against my pride, my irritability, my grumpiness, my selfishness. I need to keep short accounts now, because I may never have time to make amends or apology in this life. The Bible speaks to me about this with ever greater authority and relevance. Each day as I open it, God speaks straight into my heart by His Word. And it tells me of what lies

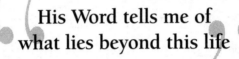

His Word tells me of what lies beyond this life

beyond this life. I can see the end of life. It looms over the horizon, and I am encouraged to think it will not now be long before I am there. As the distance between me and the finishing line decreases, I am encouraged to believe more strongly that I will make it. I know it is God's work and not mine that will get me there, but it is still reassuring to know that the time is short and the opportunity to fall into gross sin is diminishing. I have less and less chance to betray our calling in some way, and I am comforted by that thought. I have always been aware of the huge depth of depravity of my own heart and the threat that poses to me every day. Now there are many fewer days left to face that threat than I thought.

Hope in the face of death

Opportunities to tell others about Jesus have now also become clearer and more urgent. Our age is so devoid of hope in the face of death that the topic has become unmentionable. But once you have had the news I have had, it rears its head whether you want it to or not. I have learnt to go about it gently after a trip to a hairdresser in Eastbourne. The girl cutting my hair asked me how I was and I replied that I had been told that I had got just a few more months to live. I could not get another word out of her for the rest of the haircut!

But people's dread of death does not mean that they do not need to think about it, and that they are not aware that it is where every life ends.

To share the hope of eternal life is a wonderful privilege

To share the hope of eternal life is a wonderful privilege, particularly when it is apparent to the non-believer that eternal life is a reality to you, the believer. I have not done well at sharing this hope, but I am so grateful for opportunities to do it a little more boldly as my own death approaches. I have no excuse for not seizing them.

The resurrection

It has been a disappointment to discover how many fellow believers struggle to grasp the strength of our Christian hope. In the early chapters of Acts, as the first Christian sermons were being preached, they put a tremendous emphasis on the resurrection (e.g. Acts 2:24-36; 3:15; 4:2,10; 5:30; 10:39-40; 13:30; 17:2-3, 31-32). So much so, that when Paul preached in Athens, they thought he was proclaiming multiple deities — Jesus and *Anastasia* (which means resurrection, Acts 17:18)!

The resurrection plays a smaller part in contemporary gospel proclamation and that may explain why, with a good few fellow Christians, I think I have seen similar unspoken speech bubbles like the one which I saw over the surgeon's head when he first broke the news to me. They find it hard to believe that the resurrection to eternal life is a prospect to be welcomed and, like the pagan world, they assume Christians should dread death and seek to extend life at all costs.

Healing?

I do not think it entirely wrong to seek healing, but I have not particularly wanted that for myself and this has puzzled some. I have not wanted expensive courses of chemotherapy that for me could only have promised an extra few months of

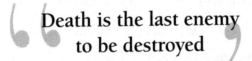

Death is the last enemy to be destroyed

life at best. I hope I am not making light of the prospect of death. It is the last enemy (1 Corinthians 15:26) and all Christians shrink naturally from it. But it is *'The last enemy to be destroyed'* and we are called to live out its destruction in our own lives and deaths as believers. In that famous chapter (1 Corinthians 15), Paul makes it clear that without belief in the resurrection, not only the deaths but also the lives of believers become a travesty: *'And if Christ has not been raised, your faith is futile; you are still in your sins. Then those also who have fallen asleep in Christ are lost. If only for this life we have hope in Christ, we are to be pitied more than all men.'*

(1 Corinthians 15:17-19).

Here is one area where Christians have a wonderful opportunity to stand out as different from our contemporary culture. Our contemporaries are obsessed with healing and the extension of

> **Christians have a wonderful opportunity to stand out**

physical life at all costs. What a pity that we Christians imitate them in that! When we talk about the hope of healing and the relief of physical pain, our contemporaries love it and they flock to our 'healing services' with high hopes. But when we talk about glory lying beyond the grave and our sure hope of eternal life, they are brought up short and are forced to face their own eternal destinies.

So it is with Christians as well as non-believers that I have tried to share the good news of resurrection. The warning of my death has brought it into much clearer perspective for me and I regret that I have not proclaimed it much more powerfully through the 37 years of my preaching ministry.

Physical trials

While this period of life is spiritually rich, it is inevitably physically depressing. For 60 years it has been customary for me, if I do not feel well, to go to sleep and know that I will wake up feeling better (or, if I do not, I just go back to sleep until I do feel better). But to know now that I will never feel better, that tomorrow will always be a little bit worse than

> **The knowledge that I have cancer never goes away**

today, is a very different experience. The knowledge that I have cancer never goes away. I am aware that I am dying every moment of every day, and every waking moment of every night. Each day is new territory for me: will I get up in the morning and find I

 Each day is new territory for me

cannot control my bowels? Or will I suddenly be hit by an unexpected fit of retching in the middle of the day? The trial is knowing that I will never feel 'better' again, and that the edge is going from all physical pleasures. For a very different reason from Hamlet, I know what he meant when he said,

> *'How weary, stale, flat and unprofitable*
> *Seem to me all the uses of this world.'*

No physical pleasures can any longer please as they once did: food, exercise, rest. Loss of appetite, bad digestion, fatigue, incontinence, cramps and the side-effects of steroids have taken their joys away. Weariness rules and physical pleasures flee. Ecclesiastes 12 is a great reminder to us that this stage of life comes to almost everyone:

> *'Remember your Creator*
> *in the days of your youth,*
> *before the days of trouble come*
> *and the years approach when you will*
> *say, "I find no pleasure in them" —'*

> *(Ecclesiastes 12:1).*

Life's joys

Having the pleasure taken out of so many of life's joyful experiences reminds us that they were all a gift to us in the first place. I never had a right to them. They never belonged to me. And I need to remember the Giver.

Ecclesiastes goes on:

'Remember him — before the silver cord is severed, or the golden bowl is broken; before the pitcher is shattered at the spring, or the wheel broken at the well, and the dust returns to the ground it came from, and the spirit returns to God who gave it.

(Ecclesiastes 12:6-7).

All the things of earth will soon be gone forever and I have a sense of savouring some of them especially because of that. I realise it may be the last time I watch a fireworks display or see a particular country view. The added poignancy makes me want to thank God even more for them, and makes me sorry that I have so often taken them for granted.

But more than all the rich experience of material things on earth, I realise that it is relationships

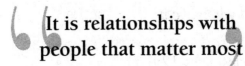

It is relationships with people that matter most

with people that matter most. A kind cousin suggested that he and I revisit the River Cothi in Carmarthenshire, where our family used to fish for some 25 years. As it turned out, I was ill on the dates we had planned for the visit and it had to be cancelled. But a visit to those cousins was still possible later, and I realised that I actually wanted to renew my acquaintance with the cousins far more than I wanted to

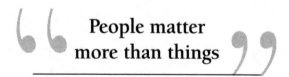

People matter more than things

walk again on the banks of that lovely and exciting river, with all its magical memories from my youth. People do matter more than things, and it will be leaving people that will hurt most at death.

Death – a devastating barrier

There is no question about the savagery of death in this regard. There is no more devastating a barrier in all of human experience than that between the living and the dead. The soft soap and wishful thinking peddled by false prophets in the face of death (that the loved one is 'just in the next room', that he's 'looking down on us all the time', that she'll be 'invisibly present at every family gathering') are iniquitous because they fly in the face of all human experience of death, and have no basis in the word of God.

The Bible is clear that *'it is appointed to man once to die and after that comes*

He is the only hope we have

judgement' (Hebrews 9:27 RSV). Every one of us will face up to God to answer for our lives, and every one of us will hang our heads in shame as we realize that we have to be condemned for the way we have lived in God's world as if it was our own world. But, even as my condemnation is announced, my Redeemer will rise at last (Job 19:25), and Jesus will present incontrovertible evidence that my sentence has been fully carried out when he died in my place on the cross. It is my relationship with him that can take me through death and which is the only hope we have of eternal life. He alone is the destroyer of death.

The one relationship

So, despite the very great strength of human love (Song of Solomon 8:12), it cannot destroy death. There

> **There is only one relationship that can destroy death...**

is only one relationship that can do that. And it is the relationship that stands behind all other relationships. In this whole experience I have drawn so much strength from my relationship with my wife (God's best gift to me after Jesus, and one that has got better and better despite all my sin), and from my relationships with my three children (and three wonderful children-in-law). They have been pillars of spiritual strength to me and I have rejoiced to watch the children grow past me in their faith. Their (and their mother's) faith has been their greatest gift to me. But then I realise it is not actually their gift to me, but God's gift to them; and so his gift to me via them. He is the relationship that stands behind all relationships.

So it is in terms of relating to him that I must understand my death. Jesus will be the same — indeed, he will be more real and more true than he has ever been before. It will be his voice that will call me into his presence (1 Thessalonians 4:16). He will himself take me to be with him (John 14:3), so that I may be with him forever (1 Thessalonians 4:17). He is the first and the last (Revelation 1:17-18), the beginning and the end (Revelation 21:6). It has been said that, for the believer, the end of the world is more of a person than it is an event. That is

> **The end of the world is more of a person than it is an event**

certainly true of the end of life. My death may be the event with which my physical life on earth ends, but it will also be the moment at which my relationship with Jesus becomes complete. That relationship is the only thing that has made sense of my physical life, and at my death it will be everything.

The first resurrection

The first Christian believers were adamant that the resurrection of Jesus Christ from the dead was God's reversal of the verdict we humans pass on Jesus: "… *you, with the help of wicked men, put him to death by nailing him to the cross. But God raised him from the dead, freeing him from the agony of death, because it was impossible for death to keep its hold on him.*" (Acts 2:23-24). Men passed their verdict. God reversed it by passing his. Without the resurrection, we would not know of that reversal. It was God's definitive act to approve Jesus' life and death. It said to everyone, "This man is

God's Son and has done what God sent him to do."

⌇

But that was 2,000 years ago, and how can I grasp the resurrection in

> **My own death asks me the question: is this the end, or not?**

the same way that they could? If I had been alive then, I could have sat down with an eyewitness and cross-questioned him or her. I can't do that now. But I do have my own death, asking me the question: is this the end, or not? Am I going out into the night and extermination, making all I have done on earth quite meaningless? Or is there something beyond the grave? Is there a life after life, which will iron out all the deficiencies of our present existence?

Jesus has risen

My death forces me to face the resurrection of Jesus. No longer is it a bald fact of history for me. It is of crucial significance for every person

> **My death forces me to face the resurrection of Jesus**

who faces their own death honestly. Until I am dead, I cannot know what will happen to me after my death. But Jesus has already risen. If I know him now, I will know him then. He is my assurance in dying, and his resurrection is central to Christianity.

Love for sinners

We all die as great sinners saved by the great grace of a far greater God. Funeral eulogies rarely present an honest picture of a person's life. The good is magnified, the bad excluded. But when Christians are remembered as they really were: including their failures and follies, their bad moods and intolerance, their moments of harshness and unkindness, then Christ is made more glorious. For he is the one who has saved us despite our sin; who has loved us even in our weakness. Our salvation is not the record of our deeds on earth, but the intervening action of a loving God, who has saved us despite who we are and what we've done. And, if he can save us, then he can save anyone!

That is why it is so important to be realistic and to be biblical about death. In dying, I want to say to those I have loved and to those who have loved me: "Don't magnify me — remember the reality: I was someone

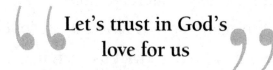

> **Let's trust in God's love for us**

who sometimes got you cross, and irritated you, and let you down, and disappointed you, and hurt you. So please don't remember an imaginary relationship with me. It was good, but it could have been better. I loved you, but I could have loved you better — just as you loved me, but you could have loved me better. So don't let's trust in our love for one another. Let's trust in God's love for us so that the change in our relationship, which my death will bring, can strengthen each of our relationships with Jesus."

My prayer

It is my prayer for my family and friends, that my death will be for them all a great strengthening and clarifying of their relationship with Jesus.

Amen.

Mark Ashton was the vicar of St Andrew the Great in Cambridge for 23 years. He became a Christian at the age of 20 while a student at Oxford. He was married to Fiona, father to Chris, Clare and Nick, and grandfather to Caleb.

Mark was diagnosed with inoperable gallbladder cancer in December 2008. During the following 15 months, as he had since his conversion, Mark wanted to share the good news of Jesus with everyone he met. He faced his imminent death with confidence — and even anticipation — because of his trust in the risen Jesus. Mark died peacefully with his family beside him in April 2010.

Towards the end, when his speech was restricted to the occasional word or two, he repeatedly said the words, 'Soon home'.